A MESSAGE FROM GOD

LIGHT LIVING IN DARK DAYS

by

PAM GILLASPIE

Dedicated to . . .

Dave
You always put up with me and you always encourage me to be
all that God intended me to be. I love you!

Scripture taken from the
NEW AMERICAN STANDARD BIBLE®,
© Copyright 1960, 1962, 1963, 1968, 1971, 1972, 1973, 1975, 1977, 1995
by The Lockman Foundation.
Used by permission. (www.Lockman.org)

A Message From God: Light Living in Dark Days

Copyright © 2026 by Pam Gillaspie
Published by Ignite Bible Ministries
www.pamgillaspie.com

ISBN 978-1-960938-14-5

Printed in the United States of America

2026

A
MESSAGE
FROM
GOD

Life happens. Whether it's family or church, job or kids, sickness or health, busyness or loneliness, life is filled with unpredictable elements, with variables that lift us up one day only to come crashing down like waves over a ship's bow the next. Life happens.

In the midst of life happening, even the best intentions can run aground. Optimism says "Not me!" but we live in a broken world that both theologians and actuaries can tell you will eventually disappoint even the half-fulls among us.

Flexible inductive studies are designed with hopeful reality in mind! The main portion of the study offers flexibility enough to bend to each week's demands (and surprises!) and the *Extras!* section at the end of each lesson invites those with different learning styles—and the occasional gift of more time!—to try some new ways of remembering the lesson.

When life happens, don't drop your Bible . . . hold it more tightly and flex!

Enjoy!

How to use this study

Flexible Inductive Studies meet you where you are and take you as far as you want to go.

1. **WEEKLY STUDY:** The main text guides you through the complete topic of study for each lesson.

2. **FYI boxes:** For Your Information boxes provide bite-sized material to shed additional light on the topic.

3. **ONE STEP FURTHER and other sidebar boxes:** Sidebar boxes give you the option to push yourself a little further. If you have extra time or are looking for an extra challenge, you can try one, all, or any number in between! These boxes give you the ultimate in flexibility.

4. **DIGGING DEEPER boxes:** If you're looking to go further, Digging Deeper sections will help you sharpen your skills as you continue to mine the truths of Scripture for yourself.

CONTENTS

LESSON ONE
The Message from God 1

LESSON TWO
Walk this Way 23

LESSON THREE
Abide in Him 39

LESSON FOUR
Children of God 53

LESSON FIVE
Believe in Jesus! 65

LESSON SIX
Getting Past "Really?" 77

LESSON SEVEN
So You May Know 93

Resources 109

LESSON ONE
1 John 1: The Message from God

*This is the message we have heard from Him and
announce to you, that God is Light, and in Him
there is no darkness at all.*
—1 John 1:5

What would you have done if you had received a message from God as
the Apostle John did? We know what he did—he wrote it down to tell
everyone what it meant for him and for the entire world! It is a message
he faithfully proclaimed and still today people around the world continue
to declare it—that God is Light and has no darkness at all. Let's look for
ourselves!

A Letter From an Apostle

Although this letter claims no author, most scholars believe it was written
by the Apostle John who also wrote the Gospel of John, the short letters
of 2 and 3 John, and the book of Revelation.

If You're in a Class

Work on **Lesson One** together on your first day of class. This will be a great way to start getting
to know each other!

USING AN INDUCTIVE APPROACH

As we study together, we'll use an inductive approach toward the Bible. With increases in connectivity and information technology today, we have access to study tools and resources unparalleled in history, but the main thing remains the main thing—the Bible itself. In studying inductively, the Bible (not people's commentaries on it!) is always the primary source for our study. In studying inductively, we'll learn to discover truth for ourselves.

Inductive study has three main components that we'll walk through step-by-step: *observation, interpretation,* and *application.*

Observation asks: *What does the text say?*

Interpretation asks: *What does the text mean?*

Application asks: *How can I apply this truth in my life?*

Together they lead to transformation by the Spirit through the Word.

MARKING the text of Scripture is one tool that will help us to observe the text well. We identify key words by reading carefully, then we mark them. Key words are typically repeated and critical to understanding the meaning of the text. When we identify key words, we're beginning to see what is going on in the text, what the author's main point is. As we mark key words, we ASK the 5W and H questions (*Who? What? When? Where? Why?* and *How?*).

To practice this basic skill and to help us key in on a major theme of John's letter, let's read through 1 John and MARK every occurrence of the word *know* by drawing a simple box around the word like this: know

OVERVIEW

1 John 1

1 *What was from the beginning, what we have heard, what we have seen with our eyes, what we have looked at and touched with our hands, concerning the Word of Life—*

2 *and the life was manifested, and we have seen and testify and proclaim to you the eternal life, which was with the Father and was manifested to us—*

3 *what we have seen and heard we proclaim to you also, so that you too may have fellowship with us; and indeed our fellowship is with the Father, and with His Son Jesus Christ.*

4 These things we write, so that our joy may be made complete.

5 This is the message we have heard from Him and announce to you, that God is Light, and in Him there is no darkness at all.

6 If we say that we have fellowship with Him and yet walk in the darkness, we lie and do not practice the truth;

7 but if we walk in the Light as He Himself is in the Light, we have fellowship with one another, and the blood of Jesus His Son cleanses us from all sin.

8 If we say that we have no sin, we are deceiving ourselves and the truth is not in us.

9 If we confess our sins, He is faithful and righteous to forgive us our sins and to cleanse us from all unrighteousness.

10 If we say that we have not sinned, we make Him a liar and His word is not in us.

1 John 2

1 My little children, I am writing these things to you so that you may not sin. And if anyone sins, we have an Advocate with the Father, Jesus Christ the righteous;

2 and He Himself is the propitiation for our sins; and not for ours only, but also for those of the whole world.

3 By this we know that we have come to know Him, if we keep His commandments.

4 The one who says, "I have come to know Him," and does not keep His commandments, is a liar, and the truth is not in him;

5 but whoever keeps His word, in him the love of God has truly been perfected. By this we know that we are in Him:

6 the one who says he abides in Him ought himself to walk in the same manner as He walked.

7 Beloved, I am not writing a new commandment to you, but an old commandment which you have had from the beginning; the old commandment is the word which you have heard.

8 On the other hand, I am writing a new commandment to you, which is true in Him and in you, because the darkness is passing away and the true Light is already shining.

9 The one who says he is in the Light and yet hates his brother is in the darkness until now.

10 The one who loves his brother abides in the Light and there is no cause for stumbling in him.

11 But the one who hates his brother is in the darkness and walks in the darkness, and does not know where he is going because the darkness has blinded his eyes.

12 I am writing to you, little children, because your sins have been forgiven you for His name's sake.

13 I am writing to you, fathers, because you know Him who has been from the beginning. I am writing to you, young men, because you have overcome the evil one. I have written to you, children, because you know the Father.

14 I have written to you, fathers, because you know Him who has been from the beginning. I have written to you, young men, because you are strong, and the word of God abides in you, and you have overcome the evil one.

15 Do not love the world nor the things in the world. If anyone loves the world, the love of the Father is not in him.

16 For all that is in the world, the lust of the flesh and the lust of the eyes and the boastful pride of life, is not from the Father, but is from the world.

17 The world is passing away, and also its lusts; but the one who does the will of God lives forever.

18 Children, it is the last hour; and just as you heard that antichrist is coming, even now many antichrists have appeared; from this we know that it is the last hour.

19 They went out from us, but they were not really of us; for if they had been of us, they would have remained with us; but they went out, so that it would be shown that they all are not of us.

20 But you have an anointing from the Holy One, and you all know.

21 I have not written to you because you do not know the truth, but because you do know it, and because no lie is of the truth.

22 Who is the liar but the one who denies that Jesus is the Christ? This is the antichrist, the one who denies the Father and the Son.

23 Whoever denies the Son does not have the Father; the one who confesses the Son has the Father also.

24 As for you, let that abide in you which you heard from the beginning. If what you heard from the beginning abides in you, you also will abide in the Son and in the Father.

25 This is the promise which He Himself made to us: eternal life.

26 These things I have written to you concerning those who are trying to deceive you.

27 As for you, the anointing which you received from Him abides in you, and you have no need for anyone to teach you; but as His anointing teaches you about all things, and is true and is not a lie, and just as it has taught you, you abide in Him.

28 Now, little children, abide in Him, so that when He appears, we may have confidence and not shrink away from Him in shame at His coming.

29 If you know that He is righteous, you know that everyone also who practices righteousness is born of Him.

1 John 3

1 See how great a love the Father has bestowed on us, that we would be called children of God; and such we are. For this reason the world does not know us, because it did not know Him.

2 Beloved, now we are children of God, and it has not appeared as yet what we will be. We know that when He appears, we will be like Him, because we will see Him just as He is.

3 And everyone who has this hope fixed on Him purifies himself, just as He is pure.

4 Everyone who practices sin also practices lawlessness; and sin is lawlessness.

5 You know that He appeared in order to take away sins; and in Him there is no sin.

6 No one who abides in Him sins; no one who sins has seen Him or knows Him.

7 Little children, make sure no one deceives you; the one who practices righteousness is righteous, just as He is righteous;

8 the one who practices sin is of the devil; for the devil has sinned from the beginning. The Son of God appeared for this purpose, to destroy the works of the devil.

9 No one who is born of God practices sin, because His seed abides in him; and he cannot sin, because he is born of God.

10 By this the children of God and the children of the devil are obvious: anyone who does not practice righteousness is not of God, nor the one who does not love his brother.

11 For this is the message which you have heard from the beginning, that we should love one another;

12 not as Cain, who was of the evil one and slew his brother. And for what reason did he slay him? Because his deeds were evil, and his brother's were righteous.

13 Do not be surprised, brethren, if the world hates you.

14 We know that we have passed out of death into life, because we love the brethren. He who does not love abides in death.

15 Everyone who hates his brother is a murderer; and you know that no murderer has eternal life abiding in him.

16 We know love by this, that He laid down His life for us; and we ought to lay down our lives for the brethren.

17 But whoever has the world's goods, and sees his brother in need and closes his heart against him, how does the love of God abide in him?

18 Little children, let us not love with word or with tongue, but in deed and truth.

19 We will know by this that we are of the truth, and will assure our heart before Him

20 in whatever our heart condemns us; for God is greater than our heart and knows all things.

21 Beloved, if our heart does not condemn us, we have confidence before God;

22 and whatever we ask we receive from Him, because we keep His commandments and do the things that are pleasing in His sight.

23 This is His commandment, that we believe in the name of His Son Jesus Christ, and love one another, just as He commanded us.

24 The one who keeps His commandments abides in Him, and He in him. We know by this that He abides in us, by the Spirit whom He has given us.

1 John 4

1   Beloved, do not believe every spirit, but test the spirits to see whether they are from God, because many false prophets have gone out into the world.

2   By this you know the Spirit of God: every spirit that confesses that Jesus Christ has come in the flesh is from God;

3   and every spirit that does not confess Jesus is not from God; this is the spirit of the antichrist, of which you have heard that it is coming, and now it is already in the world.

4   You are from God, little children, and have overcome them; because greater is He who is in you than he who is in the world.

5   They are from the world; therefore they speak as from the world, and the world listens to them.

6   We are from God; he who knows God listens to us; he who is not from God does not listen to us. By this we know the spirit of truth and the spirit of error.

7   Beloved, let us love one another, for love is from God; and everyone who loves is born of God and knows God.

8   The one who does not love does not know God, for God is love.

9   By this the love of God was manifested in us, that God has sent His only begotten Son into the world so that we might live through Him.

10   In this is love, not that we loved God, but that He loved us and sent His Son to be the propitiation for our sins.

11   Beloved, if God so loved us, we also ought to love one another.

12   No one has seen God at any time; if we love one another, God abides in us, and His love is perfected in us.

13   By this we know that we abide in Him and He in us, because He has given us of His Spirit.

14   We have seen and testify that the Father has sent the Son to be the Savior of the world.

15   Whoever confesses that Jesus is the Son of God, God abides in him, and he in God.

16   We have come to know and have believed the love which God has for us. God is love, and the one who abides in love abides in God, and God abides in him.

17 By this, love is perfected with us, so that we may have confidence in the day of judgment; because as He is, so also are we in this world.

18 There is no fear in love; but perfect love casts out fear, because fear involves punishment, and the one who fears is not perfected in love.

19 We love, because He first loved us.

20 If someone says, "I love God," and hates his brother, he is a liar; for the one who does not love his brother whom he has seen, cannot love God whom he has not seen.

21 And this commandment we have from Him, that the one who loves God should love his brother also.

1 John 5

1 Whoever believes that Jesus is the Christ is born of God, and whoever loves the Father loves the child born of Him.

2 By this we know that we love the children of God, when we love God and observe His commandments.

3 For this is the love of God, that we keep His commandments; and His commandments are not burdensome.

4 For whatever is born of God overcomes the world; and this is the victory that has overcome the world—our faith.

5 Who is the one who overcomes the world, but he who believes that Jesus is the Son of God?

6 This is the One who came by water and blood, Jesus Christ; not with the water only, but with the water and with the blood. It is the Spirit who testifies, because the Spirit is the truth.

7 For there are three that testify:

8 the Spirit and the water and the blood; and the three are in agreement.

9 If we receive the testimony of men, the testimony of God is greater; for the testimony of God is this, that He has testified concerning His Son.

10 The one who believes in the Son of God has the testimony in himself; the one who does not believe God has made Him a liar, because he has not believed in the testimony that God has given concerning His Son.

11 And the testimony is this, that God has given us eternal life, and this life is in His Son.

12　He who has the Son has the life; he who does not have the Son of God does not have the life.

13　These things I have written to you who believe in the name of the Son of God, so that you may know that you have eternal life.

14　This is the confidence which we have before Him, that, if we ask anything according to His will, He hears us.

15　And if we know that He hears us in whatever we ask, we know that we have the requests which we have asked from Him.

16　If anyone sees his brother committing a sin not leading to death, he shall ask and God will for him give life to those who commit sin not leading to death. There is a sin leading to death; I do not say that he should make request for this.

17　All unrighteousness is sin, and there is a sin not leading to death.

18　We know that no one who is born of God sins; but He who was born of God keeps him, and the evil one does not touch him.

19　We know that we are of God, and that the whole world lies in the power of the evil one.

20　And we know that the Son of God has come, and has given us understanding so that we may know Him who is true; and we are in Him who is true, in His Son Jesus Christ. This is the true God and eternal life.

21　Little children, guard yourselves from idols.

A CLOSER LOOK AT 1 JOHN 1

Now that we've quickly overviewed the letter, let's go back to look at it slowly, chapter by chapter, section by section.

INDUCTIVE FOCUS:

Context

Although we'll sometimes focus on portions of chapters or books of the Bible, it is always a good idea to read entire sections if you have the time. Reading the context—the material around what you're studying—will typically help you gain quicker and better understanding. This is why we're taking time to read John's entire letter prior to delving into individual sections of the text.

INDUCTIVE FOCUS:

Asking Questions of the Entire Letter

One of the most effective ways to understand the Bible, or any text you're engaging for that matter, is to read it slowly and carefully and then ask the basic investigative questions: *Who? What? When? Where? Why?* and *How?* Having read 1 John, see how you do on the following questions. We'll stay pretty basic for now. Remember, you can always ask different types of questions and many questions will involve asking follow-ups. Go back and re-read if you need to. As you continue to study, you'll find that asking these type questions as you read will become second nature to you if it isn't already.

Who's writing? Who is being written to?

What is the author writing about?

What can the readers "know" and how can they know it?
(Look back at what you've marked and make a simple list to help you answer.)

Why is the author writing?

1 John 1:1-4
OBSERVE the TEXT of SCRIPTURE

READ 1 John 1:1-4 and **MARK** every occurrence of the repeated word *what*.

1 John 1:1-4

1 *What was from the beginning, what we have heard, what we have seen with our eyes, what we have looked at and touched with our hands, concerning the Word of Life—*

2 *and the life was manifested, and we have seen and testify and proclaim to you the eternal life, which was with the Father and was manifested to us—*

3 *what we have seen and heard we proclaim to you also, so that you too may have fellowship with us; and indeed our fellowship is with the Father, and with His Son Jesus Christ.*

4 *These things we write, so that our joy may be made complete.*

DISCUSS with your GROUP or PONDER on your own . . .

Look back at all of the *"what"s* you marked in the text and make a short list to see if you can determine what John is getting at! Record the verse where you find the information. Here are a couple to get you started.

"What"
- "from the beginning" (v. 1)
- heard, seen, and touched (v. 1)

Based on your list, what or who do you think John is talking about? Explain your answer.

What does John say specifically about how long "the Word of Life" has existed and will exist? What implications does this have?

Is it important that John and others heard, saw, and touched it? From the rest of the Bible, do you think see, hear, and touch are physical actions?

Why was John so eager to proclaim what he had seen, heard, and touched? (Study the "so that" statements!)

A Look at the Gospel of John

In order to understand a little more about John's first letter, let's spend some time looking at another of his writings that centered on Jesus. Here we'll find out more about the Word of Life that was from the beginning!

INDUCTIVE FOCUS:

Cross-Referencing

Cross-referencing simply means comparing what the Bible says about a topic in different places. In 1 John, the Apostle John talks about "the Word of Life" to readers who immediately knew who he was referring to. In order for us to understand this more clearly, we can see more of his description of "the Word" in the prologue to his Gospel.

Gospel simply means "good news." So the Gospel of John is John's account of the good news about Jesus Christ.

This is the reason that we are taking a brief trip to look at a portion of the first chapter of the Gospel of John. We'll be back to John's letter soon!

OBSERVE the TEXT of SCRIPTURE

READ John 1:1-5 and **MARK** references to *the Word* including synonyms and pronouns. (Don't miss the qualities *life* and *light*.)

1 *In the beginning was the Word, and the Word was with God, and the Word was God.*

2 *He was in the beginning with God.*

3 *All things came into being through Him, and apart from Him nothing came into being that has come into being.*

4 *In Him was life, and the life was the Light of men.*

5 *The Light shines in the darkness, and the darkness did not comprehend it.*

DISCUSS with your GROUP or PONDER on your own . . .

Make a short list of everything new you learned about the Word from these verses.

Again, who is "the Word" that John talks about in his Gospel and First Epistle? How long has the Word been around?

OBSERVE the TEXT of SCRIPTURE

READ John 1:9-14, 17-18 and again **MARK** references to *the Word* including characteristics, synonyms (*the true Light, the only begotten, Jesus Christ*) and pronouns (*He, His, Him*).

9 *There was the true Light which, coming into the world, enlightens every man.*

10   He was in the world, and the world was made through Him, and the world did not know Him.

11   He came to His own, and those who were His own did not receive Him.

12   But as many as received Him, to them He gave the right to become children of God, even to those who believe in His name,

13   who were born, not of blood nor of the will of the flesh nor of the will of man, but of God.

14   And the Word became flesh, and dwelt among us, and we saw His glory, glory as of the only begotten from the Father, full of grace and truth.

17   For the Law was given through Moses; grace and truth were realized through Jesus Christ.

18   No one has seen God at any time; the only begotten God who is in the bosom of the Father, He has explained Him.

DISCUSS with your GROUP or PONDER on your own . . .

What is the Word's relationship to the world?

What did the Word give to those who received Him? What does this say about the Word's authority?

What did the Word do according to verse 14? What happened as a result?

According to verse 17, who is the Word?

Considering verse 18, why was it so important for Jesus to come to earth as a man and live among us? What are we able to learn from this?

1 John 1:5-10

As we get back to John's letter, he begins to tell his readers about "the message."

OBSERVE the TEXT of SCRIPTURE

READ 1 John 1:5-10 and **MARK** references to *sin*.

5   *This is the message we have heard from Him and announce to you, that God is Light, and in Him there is no darkness at all.*

6   *If we say that we have fellowship with Him and yet walk in the darkness, we lie and do not practice the truth;*

7   *but if we walk in the Light as He Himself is in the Light, we have fellowship with one another, and the blood of Jesus His Son cleanses us from all sin.*

8   *If we say that we have no sin, we are deceiving ourselves and the truth is not in us.*

9   *If we confess our sins, He is faithful and righteous to forgive us our sins and to cleanse us from all unrighteousness.*

10 *If we say that we have not sinned, we make Him a liar and His word is not in us.*

DISCUSS with your GROUP or PONDER on your own . . .

What is "the message" and who is it from?

How does this message compare with the one in John 1:9-14?

What does John say about people who say they know God but walk in the darkness?

According to the text, is there anyone who hasn't sinned?

What is "Fellowship"?

Perhaps the most recognizable use of the word "fellowship" in modern culture is found in the title of J.R.R. Tolkien's, *The Fellowship of the Ring*, the first volume of his epic work, *The Lord of the Rings*. In the book a group of adventurous souls band together for a common mission to destroy a ring that threatens their existence.

From the Greek word *koinos* (common), their fellowship (*koinonia*) is the common purpose of their mission. They all actively participate in this mission. In John's letter, we see that as people come to know God and have fellowship with Him they relate to one another based on their relationship with God.

Knowing God is not just assenting to a proper set of facts; it is being in relationship with Him through Jesus and in turn with one another . . . but you can't live what you don't know!

According to John, how do people walk in the light? How are their sins cleansed?

What benefits are realized by those who walk in the light?

When people claim they have not sinned, what are they saying about God? What does the statement say about them?

Why do you think people choose to deceive themselves?

Which person in the text best describes you—are you walking in the light or in the darkness? Have you confessed your sins and received the cleansing and forgiveness God offers in Jesus? Explain.

WHAT IS THE GOSPEL?
The Good News of Salvation by Grace through Faith in Jesus

John writes his letter assuming his readers know the basics of the Gospel. By showing them "before" and "after" snapshots of human lives, he gives his readers a simple diagnostic for knowing if they are truly in a saving relationship with Jesus and have been forgiven and cleansed from the sin that separated them from God.

The Bible is a big book but the core message is man's separation from God and God's grace making man's restoration possible. Here are the basic points (along with a few questions!) to keep in mind as we work our way through 1 John.

Romans 3:23

"for all have sinned and fall short of the glory of God,"

According to this text, is anyone "good enough" for God? What position does that put people in? Explain.

Romans 6:23

"For the wages of sin is death, but the free gift of God is eternal life in Christ Jesus our Lord."

According to this text, what do people earn when they sin?

What is God's free gift and where is it found?

Romans 5:8

"But God demonstrates His own love toward us, in that while we were yet sinners, Christ died for us."

According to this text, when and how did God demonstrate His love toward us? What condition were we in?

Based on Romans 6:23, why did Christ die?

Ephesians 2:8-9

"For by grace you have been saved through faith; and that not of yourselves, it is the gift of God; not as a result of works, so that no one may boast."

According to this text, what are people saved by and through?

What are people not saved by? Why?

If we could save ourselves, how would we likely behave?

@THE END OF THE DAY . . .

Take a couple of minutes to review what you've learned in this lesson and to consider if you've dragged any presuppositions into your study. We all have them and it's important for us to acknowledge them as we start out. What views are you bringing to the text that may color your opinions or discoveries? Do you believe the Bible is God's Word? Do you believe it is binding on your life? Do you have doubts about all or part of it? What questions do you need answered? Record below anything that's swirling around in your mind and, remember, God can handle your questions and through His Word He "has granted to us everything pertaining to life and godliness, through the true knowledge of Him" (2 Peter 1:3).

Now jot down your biggest application point from this lesson as well as your biggest remaining questions.

EXTRA

We can go over content and application together. We can observe, interpret, and apply the text. Goodness, I could give quizzes and tests to help you remember (of course, I won't!), but often what will help you remember best is thinking through on your own how you learn best. The truth doesn't change, but we learn different ways.

Memorizing is a great tool for me because it causes me to see more closely how a writer is framing an argument. When I'm focusing on recall, I'm more apt to see repeated words and patterns—it's just how my brain works!

You may recall a text best by making a simple outline of it . . . or sketching what you saw in it. If you have extra time, do what you need to so that you'll remember the basic content of 1 John 1. Here are some ideas:

Memorize Key Verses

1 John 1:5

> *This is the message we have heard from Him and announce to you, that God is Light, and in Him there is no darkness at all.*

1 John 1:9

> *If we confess our sins, He is faithful and righteous to forgive us our sins and to cleanse us from all unrighteousness.*

Got another? Write it down . . .

Create a Simple Outline

1 John 1:1-4 talks about . . .

1 John 1:5-10 talks about . . .

"Tweet" It

Brevity can make us think more accurately. See if you can summarize the message of 1 John 1 in 140 characters or less.

#Hashtag It

Make a hashtag for 1 John 1.

#

Memorize 1 John 1

Here are some of the patterns/repetitions I see. See what else you can find that helps *you* remember!

Significant patterns in verses 1-4
Statements about the Word of Life using "what" . . .

WHAT was from the beginning

WHAT we have heard

WHAT we have seen with our eyes

WHAT we have looked at and touched with our hands concerning the Word of Life

WHAT we have seen and heard we proclaim to you also

Significant patterns in verses 5-10
"If we" statements . . .

If we say that we have fellowship with Him

If we say that we have no sin

If we confess our sins

If we say that we have not sinned

If you're thinking about memorizing any verses or passages, check out **Scripturetyper.com** . . . desktop or app! I highly recommend this software that helps you memorize and keeps you honest by testing you on an ongoing basis!!

LESSON TWO
1 John 2a: Walk this Way

By this we know that we are in Him:
the one who says he abides in Him ought himself
to walk in the same manner as He walked.
—1 John 2:5b-6

Close to three out of every four Americans (73%) self-identify as "Christian" (http://www.pewforum.org/2012/10/09/nones-on-the-rise/). If we use Merriam-Webster to define "Christian," that means three out of every four Americans claim to believe in the teachings of Jesus Christ. That's a little hard to believe given how radically today's culture diverges from Jesus' words and ways.

John's letter brings to the forefront an issue relevant in both his day and ours. It is this: claiming to believe the teachings of Jesus is different from *knowing* Him. Claiming to know God (or anything else for that matter) doesn't make it true. So how can people know they truly know Him? John is quick to answer!

FYI:

Where did the word "Christian" come from?
". . . the disciples were first called Christians in Antioch."
—Acts 11:26.b

Start with Prayer

Before you read or study God's Word, first pray and ask God to guide you through His Spirit. Jesus says that the Spirit will lead us into all truth.

REMEMBERING

Take a few minutes to summarize what you learned in the last lesson.

1 John 2:1-14

Last lesson we began with a broad look at 1 John, taking a fly-by, if you will, to see how John's whole message fits together. Then we slowed down to look at the concise, 10-verse first chapter. This lesson may seem like we're slowing down even further since we'll only be looking at half of chapter 2, but that's only because 1 John 2 *is long!* Remember that as we slow down and look more deeply at individual chapters, we want to keep in mind what we've already learned in our overview of the letter.

OBSERVE the TEXT of SCRIPTURE

READ 1 John 2:1-6 and **MARK** every reference to *sin* and to *know.*

1 John 2:1-6

1   *My little children, I am writing these things to you so that you may not sin. And if anyone sins, we have an Advocate with the Father, Jesus Christ the righteous;*

2   *and He Himself is the propitiation for our sins; and not for ours only, but also for those of the whole world.*

3   *By this we know that we have come to know Him, if we keep His commandments.*

4 *The one who says, "I have come to know Him," and does not keep His commandments, is a liar, and the truth is not in him;*

5 *but whoever keeps His word, in him the love of God has truly been perfected. By this we know that we are in Him:*

6 *the one who says he abides in Him ought himself to walk in the same manner as He walked.*

DISCUSS with your GROUP or PONDER on your own . . .

How does John address his readers in this section?

Based on these verses, how do you think he views them? What clues do we have about his relationship with them? (Hint: Watch his use of we/our as you answer.)

INDUCTIVE FOCUS:

What is a Key Word?

A key word or phrase unlocks the meaning of a text. Key words are sometimes repeated and are critical to the message of the passage.

Throughout 1 John we'll see several key words. Some that we've already seen are *Light, darkness, sin, abide, truth,* and *love*. Did any of these words stick out to you as you were reading? Perhaps you noticed a number of others as well!

Identifying key words is a skill that develops over time, but you practice by observing carefully—so keep your eyes open. You will get it! Keep praying and keep looking.

What does he say about sin? Look back at every place you marked *sin* in the text and make a simple list.

What has John already said about sin in chapter 1? Is there anyone who hasn't sinned? How can people be cleansed from sin?

According to these verses, will sin be a part of a believer's life? Explain your answer from the text.

What characterizes a person who knows God?

Propitiation

Propitiation describes Christ's atoning sacrifice for man's sin. He is both the one who offers the sacrifice and the sacrifice itself, through which God justifies us, not because of any righteousness in us but because of His righteousness on our behalf.

Does claiming to know God or having good "God talk" mean someone actually knows God? Explain. What ramifications does your answer have in your life?

Which comes first according to John, keeping God's commandments or knowing God? Does knowing God come before keeping His commandments or are they simultaneous? Do the two verbs give us a temporal sequence (in which case I can know God and reject His commands for a time), a cause-effect relationship (knowing causes keeping), or a definition (keeping is knowing)? Why is this important?

How are people able to keep God's commandments?

What relationship do those who know God have with His commandments?

What effect does abiding in Christ have on a person's life? How does John describe it? Are you abiding? How do you know?

FYI:

Don't Be Afraid to Ask Questions

One of the keys to good Bible study is asking good questions and lots of them. The way we discover answers is by asking questions.

OBSERVE the TEXT of SCRIPTURE

READ 1 John 2:7-14 and **MARK** every reference to *commandment* (including any synonyms, e.g. *word*).

1 John 2:7-14

7 *Beloved, I am not writing a new commandment to you, but an old commandment which you have had from the beginning; the old commandment is the word which you have heard.*

8 *On the other hand, I am writing a new commandment to you, which is true in Him and in you, because the darkness is passing away and the true Light is already shining.*

9 *The one who says he is in the Light and yet hates his brother is in the darkness until now.*

10 *The one who loves his brother abides in the Light and there is no cause for stumbling in him.*

11 *But the one who hates his brother is in the darkness and walks in the darkness, and does not know where he is going because the darkness has blinded his eyes.*

12 *I am writing to you, little children, because your sins have been forgiven you for His name's sake.*

13 *I am writing to you, fathers, because you know Him who has been from the beginning. I am writing to you, young men, because you have overcome the evil one. I have written to you, children, because you know the Father.*

14 *I have written to you, fathers, because you know Him who has been from the beginning. I have written to you, young men, because you are strong, and the word of God abides in you, and you have overcome the evil one.*

DISCUSS with your GROUP or PONDER on your own . . .

How does John address his readers in this section?

How does this compare with his previous address? Does this agree with your assessment of John's relationship with his readers? Explain.

ONE STEP FURTHER:

Word Study: Abide

If you have some time see if you can locate the Greek word translated "abide" and find out where and how it is used in John's other writings and elsewhere in the New Testament. Then record your findings below. (Not sure how to do this? There are instructions on the last page of this lesson.)

What is the "new commandment" that John is writing about and has written about before? (In addition to the context here, check out John 13:34).

Why can this commandment be considered an "old commandment"? What "beginning" do you think John is referring to in verse 7? (See Leviticus 19:18, 34; Deuteronomy 6:5).

Who is "the true Light" that John refers to? How do you know this?

FYI:

John 13:34-35

A new commandment I give to you, that you love one another, even as I have loved you, that you also love one another. By this all men will know that you are My disciples, if you have love for one another.

—Jesus

FYI:

Leviticus 19:18, 19:34, and Deuteronomy 6:5

You shall not take vengeance, nor bear any grudge against the sons of your people, but you shall love your neighbor as yourself; I am the LORD.

—Leviticus 19:18

'The stranger who resides with you shall be to you as the native among you, and you shall love him as yourself, for you were aliens in the land of Egypt; I am the LORD your God.

—Leviticus 19:34

You shall love the LORD your God with all your heart and with all your soul and with all your might.

—Deuteronomy 6:5

Is it possible to be "in the Light" and hate a brother? Why/why not?

What does hating a brother say about a person?

What does the text teach about darkness? (You may want to mark the word and make a short list.)

What affect does it have on people? What is its relation to the Light?

Does John think his readers are walking in darkness? Why/why not?

How does he commend his readers for in verses 12-14?

According to this section, how can a person walk in the Light and overcome the evil one?

How are *you* doing at loving others?"Explain.

DIGGING DEEPER
Walk Like Jesus' Walked

If you're up for a challenge, spend some time in the Gospel accounts of how Jesus walked. Read from or listen to parts of the New Testament books of Matthew, Mark, Luke, and/or John to see Jesus for yourself, then record your observations below and consider this question: *How would my life be different if I walked more like Jesus walked?*

@THE END OF THE DAY . . .

Based on what we've studied so far, how and why can people be forgiven and have fellowship with God? What does Jesus have to do with this? What kind of evidence shows that a person has been forgiven and knows God? Have you confessed your sins and asked Him to forgive you?

EXTRA

MEMORIZE | TWEET | POST | DRAW | HASHTAG | ENCODE | REMEMBER

You've finished this lesson! This part really is for fun and to help you so-lidify what you've learned in the ways that best work for you. Seriously, see what is helpful here and use it; what doesn't work for you . . . leave it!

Memorize Key Verses

1 John 2:1-2

1 *My little children, I am writing these things to you so that you may not sin. And if anyone sins, we have an Advocate with the Father, Jesus Christ the righteous;*

2 *and He Himself is the propitiation for our sins; and not for ours only, but also for those of the whole world.*

Got another? Write it down . . .

"Tweet" It

Summarize the message of 1 John 2:1-14 in 140 characters or less.

#Hashtag It

Make a hashtag for 1 John 2:1-14.

#

Create a Simple Outline

1 John 2:1-2 tells us this about Jesus and our sin . . .

1 John 2:3-6 says we can know by this whether we have come to know
God or not . . .

1 John 2:7-14 talks about . . . .

OR Make your own outline of 1 John 2:1-14 from scratch!

Memorize 1 John 2:1-14

What significant patterns do you see that can help you memorize either
the whole passage or at least the significant flow? Did you notice how
often the word "writing" is repeated? What about the phrase "the one
who says"?

How to do an Online Word Study

For use with www.blueletterbible.org

1. Type in the Bible verse. Change the version to NASB. Click the "Search" button.

2. When you arrive at the next screen, you will see a "Tools" button to the left of your verse.
   Hover your mouse over the "Tools" button and select "Interlinear" to bring up concordance information.

3. Click on the Strong's number that links to the original word in Greek or Hebrew.

Clicking this number will bring up another screen that will give you a brief definition of the word as well as a list of every occurrence of the Greek word in the New Testament or Hebrew word in the Old Testament. Before running to the dictionary definition, scan places where this word is used in Scripture and examine the contexts where it is used.

LESSON THREE
1 John 2b: Abide in Him

Now, little children, abide in Him, so that when He appears,
we may have confidence and not shrink away from Him
in shame at His coming.
—1 John 2:28

John has been clear that a person who truly knows God will love fellow believers. It's impossible to divorce love for God from love for others as John has shown. In this next section he shows another impossibility. Just as it's impossible to divorce love for God from love for His people, it's impossible to marry love for God to love of the world. Jesus, for example, said it's impossible to love both God and wealth. But how do we love God and people while resisting the temptations and deceptions of our world and culture? We learn to abide.

Matthew 6:24
No one can serve two masters; for either he will hate the one and love the other, or he will be devoted to one and despise the other. You cannot serve God and wealth.

—Jesus

REMEMBERING

Take a few minutes to summarize what you learned in the last lesson.

1 John 2:15-29

OBSERVE the TEXT of SCRIPTURE

READ 1 John 2:15-17 and **MARK** every reference to *the world.*

1 John 2:15-17

15 *Do not love the world nor the things in the world. If anyone loves the world, the love of the Father is not in him.*

16 *For all that is in the world, the lust of the flesh and the lust of the eyes and the boastful pride of life, is not from the Father, but is from the world.*

17 *The world is passing away, and also its lusts; but the one who does the will of God lives forever.*

DISCUSS with your GROUP or PONDER on your own . . .

Earlier in this chapter, John affirmed that loving brothers is the hallmark sign of walking in the Light. Now he says there are things *not* to love. What are they?

How does John describe the world? What defines it according to verse 16?

INDUCTIVE FOCUS:

Make a List

Using key words to make a list will help you pay close attention to the text. In the space below make a list of everything you learned about *the world* from 1 John 2:15-17. Be sure to include references. Here's the first one to get you started.

• Believers are not to love the world, v. 15

Is there any relationship between the world and the Father? Explain.

Can a person love both the world and the Father? Why/Why not?

According to John 3:16 the Father loved (*agape*) the world. 1 John 2:15 tells believers to not love (agape) the world including the things in it. How would you reconcile these teachings?

ONE STEP FURTHER:

Read John 3

If you have some extra time, read John 3:1-21 where a leader of the Jewish people named Nicodemus talks with Jesus about spiritual matters. Read carefully and record your observations below.

What has John already told us about *his* heart for people in the world? (Think through 1 John 1.)

What is the world's future? How does this compare with the future of those who do the will of God?

Based on God's love for the people of the world and His commandment for us not to love the world (including the things in it and its lusts and pride), what kind of life pleases Him?

OBSERVE the TEXT of SCRIPTURE

READ 1 John 2:18-23 and **MARK** every reference to *antichrist(s)* and *lie/liars.*

1 John 2:18-23

18 *Children, it is the last hour; and just as you heard that antichrist is coming, even now many antichrists have appeared; from this we know that it is the last hour.*

19 *They went out from us, but they were not really of us; for if they had been of us, they would have remained with us; but they went out, so that it would be shown that they all are not of us.*

20 *But you have an anointing from the Holy One, and you all know.*

21 *I have not written to you because you do not know the truth, but because you do know it, and because no lie is of the truth.*

22 *Who is the liar but the one who denies that Jesus is the Christ? This is the antichrist, the one who denies the Father and the Son.*

23 *Whoever denies the Son does not have the Father; the one who confesses the Son has the Father also.*

DISCUSS with your GROUP or PONDER on your own . . .

How does John continue to show affection for and belief in his readers?

FYI:

What is the "anointing" John refers to?

Anointing during biblical times was done with oil and typically signified that a person was set apart for a specific task. The prophet Samuel, for example, anointed both Saul and David to be kings of Israel. As in the parable of the five wise virgins, the oil probably represents "wisdom," in the case of kings wisdom to rule (the task) *wisely*. John supports this by turning "anointing" into a gerund (*chrisma*, a verbal noun), equating this in the context to "teaching" (doctrine), and then finally identifying "the Spirit" with "the truth" in 1 John 5:6b. (See also Acts 10:38 and John 16:13.)

FYI:

He Will Guide You . . .

But when He, the Spirit of truth, comes, He will guide you into all the truth; for He will not speak on His own initiative, but whatever He hears, He will speak; and He will disclose to you what is to come.

—John 16:13

What contrasting people does John talk about in this section? How do the two groups differ?

What characterizes true believers?

What, if anything, comes to your mind when you hear the term "antichrist"?

How does John define "antichrist" here?

What does John say about the truth and lies? Can any lie be considered truth? Explain.

How specifically does John describe the liar in verse 22?

According to what we've learned so far from 1 John 1–2 and John 1, what truths do we know about the Father and the Son?

What is the only way to have a relationship with the Father?

FYI:

Getting it Right on Jesus

While many people today think that if you believe something sincerely you'll be all right, the Bible is clear that if you miss it on Jesus, you'll miss it all. Jesus is the Christ, the Messiah, the Anointed One. He is the eternal Word, the Son of God, the Savior of the world who has existed forever. Those who miss this or twist this miss the Father also. There is no getting to the Father without the Son as Jesus says in John 14:6: "I am the way, and the truth, and the life; no one comes to the Father but through Me."

DIGGING DEEPER
Abiding in the Vine

John talks extensively throughout his first epistle about abiding, but he also commits the entire 15th chapter of his Gospel to the meaning of abide. If you have time, read through John 15 and see what you can discover about abiding in the vine. Pray, read through the text and record what you learn below. Write a paragraph, make a chart, draw an illustration. Compile the information in whatever way you'd like but remember to OBSERVE the text carefully (*What does it say?*), INTERPRET the text paying close attention to context (*What does it mean?*), and APPLY the text (*How will I live what I've learned?*).

OBSERVE the TEXT of SCRIPTURE

READ 1 John 2:24-29 and **MARK** every reference to *abide*.

1 John 2:24-29

24 As for you, let that abide in you which you heard from the
    beginning. If what you heard from the beginning abides in you, you
    also will abide in the Son and in the Father.

25 This is the promise which He Himself made to us: eternal life.

26 These things I have written to you concerning those who are trying
    to deceive you.

27 As for you, the anointing which you received from Him abides in
    you, and you have no need for anyone to teach you; but as His
    anointing teaches you about all things, and is true and is not a lie,
    and just as it has taught you, you abide in Him.

28 Now, little children, abide in Him, so that when He appears, we
    may have confidence and not shrink away from Him in shame at His
    coming.

29 If you know that He is righteous, you know that everyone also who
    practices righteousness is born of Him.

DISCUSS with your GROUP or PONDER on your own . . .

What does John say his readers should have abide in them? What result
will this have? What does this say about people who bring new and shiny
teachings?

What promise do believers have from God?

What threat does John address? How will believers be able to stand against it? Do we face similar threats today? Explain.

What is the repeated command in this section? How do we do this? How will it benefit us?

Finally, what does John say we can know according to verse 29? What difference will it make?

@THE END OF THE DAY . . .

Considering everything we've looked at so far, how does John describe a Christian? How does this compare with what you've heard from many Americans? Is there a gap? If so, what is different between the two views?

Take some time to consider what you've written down and ask God to help you match your life more and more closely to the description John wrote down for us in the Word.

EXTRA

Remember, this isn't about more work or busy work. This section is to help you do some additional processing that works best for your learning style!

Memorize Key Verses

1 John 2:15-17

15 *Do not love the world nor the things in the world. If anyone loves the world, the love of the Father is not in him.*

16 *For all that is in the world, the lust of the flesh and the lust of the eyes and the boastful pride of life, is not from the Father, but is from the world.*

17 *The world is passing away, and also its lusts; but the one who does the will of God lives forever.*

Got another? Write it down . . .

Tweet It

Summarize the message of 1 John 2:15-29 in 140 characters or less.

Summarize the message of 1 John 2 in 140 characters or less.

Hashtag It

1 John 2:15-29

#

All of 1 John 2

#

Create a Simple Outline

1 John 2:15-17 warns about . . .

1 John 2:18-23 warns about . . .

1 John 2:24-29 talks about . . . .

OR Make your own outline of 1 John 2:15-29.

Memorize 1 John 2:15-29

What are some significant topics and patterns in this section? Where and how are the key words clustered? What contrasts help frame the text? What warnings and threats are given? What instructions? Use these significant topics and patterns to help you understand and recall as you memorize either the key points of the section or every verse word by word.

Sketch It

If you're a visual learner, sketch the key concepts from 1 John 1 and 2. Use additional paper or other materials if you need to!

LESSON FOUR
1 John 3a: Children of God

See how great a love the Father has bestowed on us,
that we would be called children of God; and such we are.
—1 John 3:1a

While modern culture spins a narrative that starts with the proposition
that everyone is a child of God, John writes about stark post-fall reality.
Two groups of people populate the world we live in: children of God and
children of the devil. Though sobering, this truth provides a snapshot of
why Jesus came to earth as a man—to destroy the works of the devil and
to provide a way for rebels to be reconciled to their Creator and be made
into beloved sons of God.

FYI:

Don't Forget to Pray
Just a reminder to pray before you study and to ask God to help you understand His Word by His
Spirit.

REMEMBERING

Take a few minutes to review what you've learned so far in 1 John 1 and 2 and record your biggest application points below.

1 John 3:1-10

OBSERVE the TEXT of SCRIPTURE

READ 1 John 3:1-3 and **MARK** references to *the Father* and to *children of God.*

1 John 3:1-3

1 *See how great a love the Father has bestowed on us, that we would be called children of God; and such we are. For this reason the world does not know us, because it did not know Him.*

2 *Beloved, now we are children of God, and it has not appeared as yet what we will be. We know that when He appears, we will be like Him, because we will see Him just as He is.*

3 *And everyone who has this hope fixed on Him purifies himself, just as He is pure.*

DISCUSS with your GROUP or PONDER on your own . . .

What is associated with being called "children of God"? What does this tell us about the Father's disposition toward us?

Is "children of God" more than a title? Explain.

What is the world's disposition toward "children of God"? Why?

What kind of tension does this create in your life now? How do you resolve it?

What implications does this have for the future? Do we know what God has in store for us?

What are we to do in the meantime? Why?

How does John describe everyone who has their hope fixed on Jesus?

FYI:

Using Commentaries
Commentaries are helpful tools to use after you've done your own study. A great new one-volume commentary on the Bible is *The Moody's Bible Commentary* edited by Dr. Michael Rydelnik and Dr. Michael Vanlaningham.

OBSERVE the TEXT of SCRIPTURE

All the children of God, those who have their hope fixed on Him, purify themselves, but not everyone who claims to know Him actually does.

READ 1 John 3:4-6 and **MARK** references to *sin* and *lawlessness*.

1 John 3:4-6

4 *Everyone who practices sin also practices lawlessness; and sin is lawlessness.*

5 *You know that He appeared in order to take away sins; and in Him there is no sin.*

6 *No one who abides in Him sins; no one who sins has seen Him or knows Him.*

DISCUSS with your GROUP or PONDER on your own . . .

What does John say about sin and lawlessness?

What about those who practice sin as an ongoing way of life?

FYI:

Defining Sin

In 1 John 3:4 John defines sin as "lawlessness." Since he is likely writing to an audience largely made up of Gentiles, there's no indication that he is using the word "law" in the sense of the Old Testament Law, but rather in more general terms of common moral law. There is clearly some overlap of the two (for instance both would include such things as "Don't steal") and John would certainly argue that anything validly right or wrong in common moral law is ultimately sourced in revelation. However in this more Gentile letter, John would not include in his "lawlessness" violations of Mosaic ritual commands like circumcision, sabbaths, sacrifices, washings, keeping a lamp lit in a temple, etc. which would be for the most part foreign to his readers.

What does Jesus' appearing have to do with sin?

What else does John say about Jesus and sin?

Bottom line: Can a person know Jesus and live in sin? Explain your answer.

How does this line up with what you see in the world around you?

OBSERVE the TEXT of SCRIPTURE

READ 1 John 3:7-10 and **MARK** references to *children* and to the *devil*.

1 John 3:7-10

7 *Little children, make sure no one deceives you; the one who practices righteousness is righteous, just as He is righteous;*

8 *the one who practices sin is of the devil; for the devil has sinned from the beginning. The Son of God appeared for this purpose, to destroy the works of the devil.*

9 *No one who is born of God practices sin, because His seed abides in him; and he cannot sin, because he is born of God.*

10 *By this the children of God and the children of the devil are obvious: anyone who does not practice righteousness is not of God, nor the one who does not love his brother.*

DISCUSS with your GROUP or PONDER on your own . . .

What term of endearment does John use again? How does his use of sentimental terms like this influence the message of his letter?

Does knowing that someone already believes in you help you respond better to what he or she says?

Anything we can learn from John's communication approach? If so, what?

What deception does John warn about in verse 7?

It's Greek to Me!

Since the New Testament was written in Greek, there are times when a little knowledge of the language goes a long way in helping us to understand the meaning of the text. This is sure the case here when John starts talking about practicing sin in 1 John 3. Check out "no one who is born of God practices sin" where John uses the present tense of the verb to specify continual action.

John is not talking about sinless perfection; we know that for sure based on what he said in the first chapter about everyone having sinned (1:10). True believers stumble and confess and then continue walking again in the path of righteousness because of their relationship with Jesus.

ONE STEP FURTHER:

Word Study: The Devil

He's cast as a varicolored mascot of countless high schools and universities but most people think of the devil as red and holding a pitchfork. The Bible paints another picture all together. If you have some extra time, see what you can find out about the Greek word for devil, *diabolos*. Find out what roots this noun is composed of and how it's used throughout the New Testament. Also check out the one place where its associated verb *diaballo* is used (Luke 16:1). Record your findings and observations below.

What deceptions has John already warned about in chapters 1 and 2? How do they compare?

Have you seen these deceptions? What effect do they have on the church and on those outside the church?

What does John say about the devil? Do you think people today believe in a literal devil? Why/why not? What difference does it make?

How does John say you can tell who is righteous?

What else characterizes those who practice righteousness?

Where does their righteousness come from?

Why are they not able to sin?

ONE STEP FURTHER:

Word Study: Righteousness

If you have time, see what you can discover about the Greek word translated "righteousness" in 1 John 3. What other words are related to it? How is it used elsewhere in John's writings and throughout the New Testament? How does a person "get" righteousness? See what you can find and record your observations below.

DIGGING DEEPER
Children of God

If you have some extra time this, explore more deeply what the New Testament teaches about being born again and about being children of God. John 3 and the letter to the Galatians (which talks about how people move from slaves to sons) are a couple of great places to start. Record what you discover below.

FYI:

The Way to Righteousness

For what does the Scripture say? "ABRAHAM BELIEVED GOD, AND IT WAS CREDITED TO HIM AS RIGHTEOUSNESS." Now to the one who works, his wage is not credited as a favor, but as what is due. But to the one who does not work, but believes in Him who justifies the ungodly, his faith is credited as righteousness,

—Romans 4:3-5

What about those who practice sin? What else characterizes them?

According to verse 8, why did the Son of God appear? What hope does this give to those John called "children of the devil"?

What other defining mark of a child of God does John mention in verse 10?

@THE END OF THE DAY . . .

Take a few minutes to reflect on the great love God has shown us in making us His sons and daughters. If you belong to Him, how has this reality been changing your life?

EXTRA

Remember, this is supposed to be fun! Do only what you enjoy in this section and don't let it stress you out—it's bonus material. If the chapter is the cake, consider this the frosting.

Memorize Key Verses

1 John 3:2-3

2 *Beloved, now we are children of God, and it has not appeared as yet what we will be. We know that when He appears, we will be like Him, because we will see Him just as He is.*

3 *And everyone who has this hope* fixed *on Him purifies himself, just as He is pure.*

Got another? Write it down . . .

"Tweet" It

Summarize the message of 1 John 3:1-10 in 140 characters or less.

#Hashtag It

1 John 3:1-10

#

Create a Simple Outline

1 John 3:1-3

1 John 3:4-6

1 John 3:7-10

OR Make your own outline of 1 John 3:1-10

Memorize 1 John 3:1-10

This is a relatively short passage . . . you could memorize the whole thing by doing just a little over a verse a day! Try grouping them together like this:

Day 1 — 1 John 3:1 (The Father's Great Love)

Day 2 — 1 John 3:2-3 (Children of God)

Day 3 — 1 John 3:4 (Sin = Lawlessness)

Day 4 — 1 John 3:5-6 (Appeared to Take Away Sin)

Day 5 — 1 John 3:7-8 (Make Sure No One Deceives You)

Day 6 — 1 John 3:9 (Cannot Sin if Born of God)

Day 7 — 1 John 3:10 (Children of God and of the devil are Obvious)

LESSON FIVE
1 John 3b: Believe in Jesus!

This is His commandment, that we believe in the name of His Son Jesus Christ, and love one another, just as He commanded us.
—1 John 3:23

Does your heart long to know if you belong to God? John continues to unfold for his readers how they can know they have eternal life even during difficult times when doubts creep into their hearts. Trees are known by their fruit . . . and that's our confidence, not that we've earned anything from God but rather that He's transforming us, conforming us more and more into the image of His Son.

REMEMBERING

Take some time to recall what you've learned so far in the first two and a half chapters of 1 John. You can make an outline of key thoughts or simply jot down how God's Word is challenging your thinking and actions.

1 John 3:11-24

OBSERVE the TEXT of SCRIPTURE

READ 1 John 3:11-12 and **MARK** the word *message.* **UNDERLINE** what the message is.

1 John 3:11-12

11 *For this is the message which you have heard from the beginning, that we should love one another;*

12 *not as Cain, who was of the evil one and slew his brother. And for what reason did he slay him? Because his deeds were evil, and his brother's were righteous.*

DISCUSS with your GROUP or PONDER on your own . . .

What is the message John's readers have heard from the beginning?

What biblical person does John give as a bad example? What does he tell us about him? What did he do and why?

ONE STEP FURTHER:

Cain and Abel

If you have some extra time, read the biblical account of Cain and Abel recorded in Genesis 4. Record your observations below.

In what practical ways can you show love for others?

Now think more specifically. What is one practical way you can show love for a specific person today?

OBSERVE the TEXT of SCRIPTURE

READ 1 John 3:13-15 and **MARK** the words *love* and *hates.*

1 John 3:13-15

13 *Do not be surprised, brethren, if the world hates you.*

14 *We know that we have passed out of death into life, because we love the brethren. He who does not love abides in death.*

15 *Everyone who hates his brother is a murderer; and you know that no murderer has eternal life abiding in him.*

DISCUSS with your GROUP or PONDER on your own . . .

What does John warn about in verse 13? How does this compare with Cain's actions toward his brother?

How can we prepare in advance for the world's hostility toward believers from day to day?

According to verse 14, what is one way people can know they "have passed out of death into life"?

Why is hate such a red flag? What does John equate it with? Does this remind you of anything Jesus taught? If so, what?

ONE STEP FURTHER:

Words for Love

If you have some extra time, see if you can discover the two most common Greek words translated "love" in the New Testament. Then describe how they differ.

DIGGING DEEPER
Jesus' Teaching from the Sermon on the Mount

Take some time to read Jesus' teaching in Matthew 5–7. Then, record below how John's letter reflects this teaching. Remember, John was a disciple of Someone Else!

Matthew 5

Matthew 6

Matthew 7

Summarize briefly where and how John's letter reflects Jesus' teaching in the Sermon on the Mount.

OBSERVE the TEXT of SCRIPTURE

READ 1 John 3:16-22 and **MARK** *love* and *truth.*

1 John 3:16-22

16 *We know love by this, that He laid down His life for us; and we ought to lay down our lives for the brethren.*

17 *But whoever has the world's goods, and sees his brother in need and closes his heart against him, how does the love of God abide in him?*

18 *Little children, let us not love with word or with tongue, but in deed and truth.*

19 *We will know by this that we are of the truth, and will assure our heart before Him*

20 *in whatever our heart condemns us; for God is greater than our heart and knows all things.*

21 *Beloved, if our heart does not condemn us, we have confidence before God;*

22 *and whatever we ask we receive from Him, because we keep His commandments and do the things that are pleasing in His sight.*

DISCUSS with your GROUP or PONDER on your own . . .

How does our culture define love?

Who taught us what love truly is? How did He teach it? What can we learn about how to love from Jesus' example?

Why are followers of Christ able to love? What powers it?

How can believers know that they are "of the truth" and assure their hearts?

What are some reasons our hearts condemn us? Are condemning hearts sovereign over God?

What are some ways others have shown you the kind of love John describes?

ONE STEP FURTHER:

When the Heart Condemns

If you have some extra time, look a little closer at verses 3:19-22. Make sure you consider the questions below, pay close attention to context, and then consult a commentary or two to compare. Finally, summarize how you can deal with your heart when it condemns you!

Here are some specific questions to consider: Where else is the word *kataginosko* (condemned) used in the New Testament? What root words make up this compound word and how are they typically translated? What verb tense does John use in verse 19? How does this relate to what he was just talking about? When John talks about the heart, is he just preaching "at" his readers or do you think he is preaching to himself also? How do you know? Does this affect meaning? If so, how? Is John talking about sinless perfection? How do you know? How does 1 John 3:19-22 relate to the main point of 1 John?

How can you deal with a heart that condemns you?

OBSERVE the TEXT of SCRIPTURE

READ 1 John 3:23-24 and **MARK** every form of *command*. Also **MARK** *abides*.

1 John 3:23-24

23 This is His commandment, that we believe in the name of His Son Jesus Christ, and love one another, just as He commanded us.

24 The one who keeps His commandments abides in Him, and He in him. We know by this that He abides in us, by the Spirit whom He has given us.

DISCUSS with your GROUP or PONDER on your own . . .

According to verse 23, what does God command people? How does this primary commandment relate to others?

Answer the following questions, then summarize how they relate to one another:

• What do we know about the one who keeps God's commandments?

• How do we know that His Spirit abides in us?

• What do we know about mankind's ability to keep God's commandments unaided?

The Greatest Commandment

But when the Pharisees heard that Jesus had silenced the Sadducees, they gathered themselves together. One of them, a lawyer, asked Him a question, testing Him, "Teacher, which is the great commandment in the Law?"

And He said to him, " 'YOU SHALL LOVE THE LORD YOUR GOD WITH ALL YOUR HEART, AND WITH ALL YOUR SOUL, AND WITH ALL YOUR MIND.' "This is the great and foremost commandment. "The second is like it, 'YOU SHALL LOVE YOUR NEIGHBOR AS YOURSELF.' "On these two commandments depend the whole Law and the Prophets."

—Matthew 22:34-40

What difference does knowing Jesus make in *your* life?

If knowing Jesus were a punishable offense, what evidence could the prosecution bring forward to convict you?

@THE END OF THE DAY . . .

Spend some time praying and thinking through what you've learned in this lesson about believers' love. Jot down the key principle you need to remember. Don't forget, sometimes less is more. #brevity

EXTRA

MEMORIZE | TWEET | POST | DRAW | HASHTAG | ENCODE | REMEMBER

It's time to review what you've done! Take your time, have fun, and maybe try a new review tool!

Memorize Key Verses

1 John 3:14 and 23

14 We know that we have passed out of death into life, because we love the brethren. He who does not love abides in death.

23 This is His commandment, that we believe in the name of His Son Jesus Christ, and love one another, just as He commanded us.

Got another? Write it down . . .

Now, jot down the verses you've memorized to this point.

°Tweet It

Summarize the message of 1 John 3:11-24 in 140 characters or less.

Hashtag It

1 John 3:11-24 . . . . .

#

Now, using hashtags, tell the main flow of 1 John so far.

1 John 1

#

1 John 2

#

1 John 3

#

Create a Simple Outline

1 John 3:11-12

1 John 3:13-15

1 John 3:16-22

OR Make your own outline of 1 John 3:11-22

Memorize 1 John 3:11-22

When I was a child, I memorized for trophies. I'm not proud of this motive, but God did His work in spite of me. You might want to try my all-time go-to strategy for memorizing. It is simple. Write the verse or verses you are memorizing on a piece of paper with light handwriting and in pencil. Then erase one or two words and read the verse or verses again supplying the missing words from memory. Continuing erasing and continue reading (preferably out loud) until you have it. Then, do it again and continue to review.

The Scripture Typer app uses a similar approach but with typing. I highly recommend it.

LESSON SIX

1 John 4: Getting Past "Really?"
AKA ... Don't Believe Everything You Hear!

Beloved, do not believe every spirit, but test the spirits to see whether they are from God, because many false prophets have gone out into the world.
—1 John 4:1

Jesus clearly called people to whole-heartedly believe He's the Son of God, but He also warned His followers not to be taken in by charlatans and deceivers who would seek to destroy them. He went so far as to instruct them to be as shrewd as snakes because He knew they would face enemies who were trying to eat them alive. Living as sheep among wolves is dangerous business but Jesus told His followers how to survive and thrive: "Behold, I send you out as sheep in the midst of wolves; so be shrewd as serpents and innocent as doves."

REMEMBERING

Briefly summarize the basics from each chapter we've studied so far and add your biggest application action items. Remember, if we're just observing and interpreting we're missing the end goal of applying the Word. We need always to apply to *our* lives the truths that we're learning!

	Main Truths/Key Words **#Hashtags!**	**My Application**
1 John 1		
1 John 2		
1 John 3		

FYI:

Don't Believe Everyone!

Be of sober spirit, be on the alert. Your adversary, the devil, prowls around like a roaring lion, seeking someone to devour.

−1 Peter 5:8

OBSERVE the TEXT of SCRIPTURE

READ 1 John 4:1-6 and **MARK** every reference to *spirit* including pronouns and synonyms.

1 John 4:1-6

1 Beloved, do not believe every spirit, but test the spirits to see whether they are from God, because many false prophets have gone out into the world.

2 By this you know the Spirit of God: every spirit that confesses that Jesus Christ has come in the flesh is from God;

3 and every spirit that does not confess Jesus is not from God; this is the spirit of the antichrist, of which you have heard that it is coming, and now it is already in the world.

4 You are from God, little children, and have overcome them; because greater is He who is in you than he who is in the world.

5 They are from the world; therefore they speak as from the world, and the world listens to them.

6 We are from God; he who knows God listens to us; he who is not from God does not listen to us. By this we know the spirit of truth and the spirit of error.

DISCUSS with your GROUP or PONDER on your own . . .

Looking back to 1 John 3:23, what two commands of Jesus does John remind his readers of?

What two commands does John make in 1 John 4:1?

Faith/Believe

The English words "faith" and "believe" come from the same Greek root (*pistis/pisteuo*). John tends to use the verb. When looking across his writings, he uses the noun "faith" (*pistis*) only 5 times while he uses the verb "believe" (*pisteuo*) a whopping 107 times.

How do these two commands relate to each other?

Are you ever perplexed as to whether a particular teaching is from God or not? If so, what throws you off? How do you usually respond when you're feeling in the twilight zone?

What does John say is a test for knowing if a spirit or teaching is from God? How can you apply this test to a life situation?

If a teaching or spirit fails this test, is it benign? Why/why not?

According to the text, do we have to fear those who fail the test? Why/ why not?

Who listens to those who fail this test? Why do they listen?

Based on these verses, how can you differentiate the spirit of truth from the spirit of error?

ONE STEP FURTHER:

Word Study: Test

If you have some extra time, see what you can discover about the Greek verb for "test" (*dokimazo*). While you're researching you may find it helpful to examine the related Greek noun *dokimos* (found in 2 Timothy 2:15) which is translated "approved." Record your findings below.

OBSERVE the TEXT of SCRIPTURE

READ 1 John 4:7-12 and **MARK** every occurrence of *love* (and forms of the word—*loves, loved, beloved*) and *God*.

The Greek word John uses for "love" is quite unique to the biblical text; in fact it is rarely used in pre-biblical Greek literature. *Agape* is a love that seeks God's best for a person. God is love and those who abide in Him love as He loves!

1 John 4:7-12

7 *Beloved, let us love one another, for love is from God; and everyone who loves is born of God and knows God.*

8 *The one who does not love does not know God, for God is love.*

9 *By this the love of God was manifested in us, that God has sent His only begotten Son into the world so that we might live through Him.*

10 *In this is love, not that we loved God, but that He loved us and sent His Son to be the propitiation for our sins.*

11 *Beloved, if God so loved us, we also ought to love one another.*

12 *No one has seen God at any time; if we love one another, God abides in us, and His love is perfected in us.*

DISCUSS with your GROUP or PONDER on your own . . .

Using your markings as a guide, make a list of everything 1 John 4:7-12 teaches about *God*.

How does John specifically describe God in verse 8? How has God shown His love toward us?

Now list everything John says about *love* in this section.

What characterizes God's love? How does it behave? What did it "cost" God? Who does it benefit?

Why are believers commanded to love? How can we practically accomplish it?

If a person does not love, what does this say about him (or her)?

How does the *agape* John writes about differ from the world's definitions of love?

OBSERVE the TEXT of SCRIPTURE

READ 1 John 4:13-16 and **MARK** references to *abide* and *love*.

1 John 4:13-16

13 By this we know that we abide in Him and He in us, because He has
    given us of His Spirit.

14 We have seen and testify that the Father has sent the Son to be the
    Savior of the world.

15 Whoever confesses that Jesus is the Son of God, God abides in him,
    and he in God.

16 We have come to know and have believed the love which God has
    for us. God is love, and the one who abides in love abides in God,
    and God abides in him.

DISCUSS with your GROUP or PONDER on your own . . .

Up to this point in his letter, how has John said a person can know that he
has come to know God?

According to verse 13 how can you know *you* abide in Him? What demonstrates this reality?

What truth will those who have the Spirit testify and confess?

How does this assure us?

DIGGING DEEPER
The Good Samaritan

Take some time to see what Jesus has to say about who our "neighbor" is. You'll find the familiar parable of the Good Samaritan in Luke 10:25-37. After you've read it through, consider who your "neighbor"s are.

OBSERVE the TEXT of SCRIPTURE

READ 1 John 4:17-21 and **MARK** references to *love* and *fear.*

1 John 4:17-21

17 *By this, love is perfected with us, so that we may have confidence in the day of judgment; because as He is, so also are we in this world.*

18 *There is no fear in love; but perfect love casts out fear, because fear involves punishment, and the one who fears is not perfected in love.*

19 *We love, because He first loved us.*

20 *If someone says, "I love God," and hates his brother, he is a liar; for the one who does not love his brother whom he has seen, cannot love God whom he has not seen.*

21 *And this commandment we have from Him, that the one who loves God should love his brother also.*

DISCUSS with your GROUP or PONDER on your own . . .

Looking back at your markings, list everything John says about love in this section.

When John says "By this, love is perfected with us," what is he referring to? (Hint: Look for the key word "this" refers to in the previous section!)

When love is perfected in a person, what results does it produce?

What does fear involve and why can't it co-exist with perfect love?

Why are believers even *able* to love at all?

According to verse 20, is love more than just a verbal declaration? Explain.

What does God command in verse 21? How are you doing at this?

ONE STEP FURTHER:

Word Study: Perfect

John tells us that perfect love casts out all fear! That's a great thing if you have perfect love . . . but it sure sounds like a tall order! If you have some time, see what you can find out about the Greek word *teleios* that the NASB has translated "perfect." I think you'll be encouraged!! Record your findings below.

@THE END OF THE DAY . . .

Take some time to reflect on what we've studied so far in these first four chapters of 1 John and record first what the most significant change to your thinking has been. Then, consider how that change to your thinking has been affecting your behavior.

EXTRA

MEMORIZE | TWEET | POST | DRAW | HASHTAG | ENCODE | REMEMBER

Some more opportunities to review and remember!

Memorize Key Verses

1 John 4:10-11, 18-19

10   *In this is love, not that we loved God, but that He loved us and sent His Son to be the propitiation for our sins.*

11   *Beloved, if God so loved us, we also ought to love one another.*

18   *There is no fear in love; but perfect love casts out fear, because fear involves punishment, and the one who fears is not perfected in love.*

19   *We love, because He first loved us.*

Got another? Write it down . . .

"Tweet" It

Summarize the message of 1 John 4 in 140 characters or less.

#Hashtag It

1 John 4

#

Create a Simple Outline

1 John 4:1-6

1 John 4:7-14

1 John 4:15-21

OR Make your own outline of 1 John 4

Memorize 1 John 4 . . .

Even if you're not memorizing the whole letter, 1 John 4:7-21 is a great stand-alone passage on love to know!

My most-used memorizing strategy as an adult has been recording myself reading a passage (with heavy inflection to give it rhythm) and then listening to the recording until I can recite it along with "myself." If you have kids or grandkids who love having the same story read over and over, you know how this works.

Once you've heard something enough times, particularly with rhythm or cadence, it sticks . . . like this one: "The sun did not shine it was too wet to play, so we sat in the house all that cold, cold wet day . . . ." — it's been years since I've read Dr. Seuss's *The Cat in the Hat,* but that came right out of my head and I could keep going because I've heard myself so many times! How much better to have "Beloved, if God so loved us, we also ought to love one another" stuck in your noggin?

Sketch It

Break out the pencils and sketch the key concepts in 1 John 3 and 4. You know, you can have fun with this even if you're not an artist . . . maybe *especially* if you're not an artist!

LESSON SEVEN
John 5: So You May Know!

These things I have written to you who believe in the name of
the Son of God, so that you may know that you have
eternal life.
—1 John 5:13

There is no deeper heart issue than this: what happens when I die? Most people wonder, many fear, but John says you and I can know that we have eternal life! Who wouldn't want to take God up on an offer like this?!

REMEMBERING

Take a few minutes to summarize 1 John 1–4. Include a theme for each chapter and a one- or two-sentence summary.

1 John 1

1 John 2

1 John 3

1 John 4

1 John 5
OBSERVE the TEXT of SCRIPTURE

READ 1 John 5:1-5 and **MARK** *believes/faith* and *overcomes/victory.*

1 John 5:1-5

1 *Whoever believes that Jesus is the Christ is born of God, and whoever loves the Father loves the child born of Him.*

2 *By this we know that we love the children of God, when we love God and observe His commandments.*

3 *For this is the love of God, that we keep His commandments; and His commandments are not burdensome.*

4 *For whatever is born of God overcomes the world; and this is the victory that has overcome the world—our faith.*

5 *Who is the one who overcomes the world, but he who believes that Jesus is the Son of God?*

DISCUSS with your GROUP or PONDER on your own . . .

According to John, how can we know who is "born of God"?

What does the phrase "Jesus is the Christ" mean? What does the name Jesus mean? What does Christ mean?

If we love the Father, how will we relate to His children and His commandments? How are you doing with this practically? What's hard and why?

How does John describe God's commandments?

ONE STEP FURTHER:

Word Study: Overcomes

If you have some extra time, see what you can discover about the Greek word translated "overcomes" and the related word translated "victory." Here's a hint: you've probably owned a pair of shoes that harken back to this Greek word . . . Michael Jordan certainly has!

Who does John say "overcomes the world" and how?

Are you living like an overcomer or one who has been overcome? Why?

OBSERVE the TEXT of SCRIPTURE

READ 1 John 5:6-12 and **MARK** the word *testify/testimony.*

1 John 5:6-12

6 *This is the One who came by water and blood, Jesus Christ; not with the water only, but with the water and with the blood. It is the Spirit who testifies, because the Spirit is the truth.*

7 *For there are three that testify:*

8 *the Spirit and the water and the blood; and the three are in agreement.*

9 *If we receive the testimony of men, the testimony of God is greater; for the testimony of God is this, that He has testified concerning His Son.*

10 *The one who believes in the Son of God has the testimony in himself; the one who does not believe God has made Him a liar, because he has not believed in the testimony that God has given concerning His Son.*

11 *And the testimony is this, that God has given us eternal life, and this life is in His Son.*

12 *He who has the Son has the life; he who does not have the Son of God does not have the life.*

DISCUSS with your GROUP or PONDER on your own . . .

How does John say Jesus came in verse 6?

What are the three things that testify?

While there is some variety of interpretation on what John is referring to by "the water and the blood," the phrase certainly confirms the historicity of Jesus. I think the "water" refers to Jesus' baptism at the outset of His public ministry; others have associated it either with His physical birth . . . or death, when His body issued "blood and water" (John 19:34). *Every one of these interpretations entails a real human being, an empirical history.* Check out the following verses.

Read Matthew 3:13-17 and briefly summarize what happens.

Read Matthew 27:1-26, briefly summarize what happens, and note where "blood" is used in the text.

Read Romans 8:16-17. What do these verses say about the Spirit?

Who else does John say testifies? What is the testimony and why is it so great?

How do people respond to the testimony and what are the results?

What is the only way to have "the life" (v. 12)? What do you have to have in order to have *this* life?

OBSERVE the TEXT of SCRIPTURE

READ 1 John 5:13-17 and **MARK** every occurrence of *know*.

1 John 5:13-17

13 *These things I have written to you who believe in the name of the Son of God, so that you may know that you have eternal life.*

14 *This is the confidence which we have before Him, that, if we ask anything according to His will, He hears us.*

15 *And if we know that He hears us* in *whatever we ask, we know that we have the requests which we have asked from Him.*

16 *If anyone sees his brother committing a sin not* leading *to death, he shall ask and* God *will for him give life to those who commit sin not* leading *to death. There is a sin* leading *to death; I do not say that he should make request for this.*

17 *All unrighteousness is sin, and there is a sin not* leading *to death.*

DISCUSS with your GROUP or PONDER on your own . . .

Who has John been writing to? What do they believe?

Why did John write according to verse 13? What does he want his readers to know for sure?

ONE STEP FURTHER:

More on Prayer

For some more on prayer, check out Jesus' teaching in Matthew 6:5-16 and Paul's in Romans 8:26-28. Record your findings below.

Do you know this for sure, now that you've studied this letter? Explain.

What other confidence can believers have? Does this mean we can get anything we want from God? Why/why not? Explain. Feel free to use cross-references if you have the time and energy.

If we see a fellow brother or sister in Christ sinning, what does John say we should do? Based on what we've seen so far in 1 John, what kind of "death" does John have in mind when he says "there is a sin not leading to death"?

What people has John described as heading toward death? How do we know they are heading there? Who have they rejected?

FYI:

Colossians 1:13-14

For He rescued us from the domain of darkness, and transferred us to the kingdom of His beloved Son, in whom we have redemption, the forgiveness of sins.

How is anyone moved from death to life? What sin is everyone committing who remains in death?

OBSERVE the TEXT of SCRIPTURE

READ 1 John 5:18-21 and again **MARK** every occurrence of *know* and every reference to *God*.

1 John 5:18-21

18 *We know that no one who is born of God sins; but He who was born of God keeps him, and the evil one does not touch him.*

19 *We know that we are of God, and that the whole world lies in the power of the evil one.*

20 *And we know that the Son of God has come, and has given us understanding so that we may know Him who is true; and we are in Him who is true, in His Son Jesus Christ. This is the true God and eternal life.*

21 *Little children, guard yourselves from idols.*

DISCUSS with your GROUP or PONDER on your own . . .

According to these verses, what do we "know"?

What does God do for the one who is born of Him?

What is the ongoing condition of the world?

How is it that anyone comes to know the true God? Do you know Him? How do you know?

What is John's final warning to his "little children"? How are you doing with this?

Finally, if someone were to ask you how to have a relationship with God, how would you answer?

@THE END OF THE DAY . . .

Take some time to think back through everything you've learned from John's letter. What truth has impacted you most? How is it changing the way you think and act? How is *your life* a witness to God's message?

As this class comes to a close, what are you planning next to pursue God through His Word?

EXTRA

Just a quick reminder to keep reviewing what you've already learned!

Memorize Key Verses

1 John 5:13

13 These things I have written to you who believe in the name of the Son of God, so that you may know that you have eternal life.

Got another? Write it down . . .

"Tweet" It

Summarize the message of 1 John 5 in 140 characters or less.

Then, summarize the message of all of 1 John in 140 characters or less!

#Hashtag It

1 John 5:

#

What's your hashtag for all of 1 John?

#

Create a Simple Outline

1 John 5:1-5

1 John 5:6-12

1 John 5:13-17

1 John 5:18-21

OR Make your own outline of 1 John 5: . . . .

Memorize 1 John 5 . . .

As you memorize 1 John 5, look for these groupings of key repeated words and phrases to help you remember.

1 John 5:1-5 — love (5x), commandments (3x), overcomes/victory (4x), faith/believes (3x)

1 John 5:6-12 — testify/testimony (10x) -- one of these you'll have to use blueletterbible.org to find since the Greek term's sound more closely corresponds to another English word.

1 John 5:13-17 — know (3x), ask/request (5x), sin not leading to death (3x)

1 John 5:18-21 – know (4x), born of God (2x)

The final memorizing tip I have for you is this: recite to someone else. I know it's hard but when someone else is listening to you, they can encourage you in your efforts and give you appropriate prompts as you practice.

Sketch It

Sketch the key concepts from 1 John 5 and then see if you can make one sketch that summarizes the whole letter.

Resources

Helpful Study Tools

The New How to Study Your Bible
Eugene, Oregon: Harvest House
Publishers

The New Inductive Study Bible
Eugene, Oregon: Harvest House
Publishers

Logos Bible Software
Available at www.logos.com.

Greek Word Study Tools

Kittel, G., Friedrich, G., &
Bromiley, G.W.
*Theological Dictionary of the New
Testament, Abridged* (also known
as Little Kittel)
Grand Rapids, Michigan: W.B.
Eerdmans Publishing Company

Zodhiates, Spiros
*The Complete Word Study
Dictionary:
New Testament*
Chattanooga, Tennessee:
AMG Publishers

Hebrew Word Study Tools

Harris, R.L., Archer, G.L., &
Walker, B.K.
*Theological Wordbook of the
Old Testament* (also known as
TWOT)
Chicago, Illinois: Moody Press

Zodhiates, Spiros
*The Complete Word Study
Dictionary: Old Testament*
Chattanooga, Tennessee:
AMG Publishers

General Word Study Tools

Strong, James
*The New Strong's Exhaustive
Concordance of the Bible*
Nashville, Tennessee:
Thomas Nelson

Recommended Commentary Sets

Expositor's Bible Commentary
Grand Rapids, Michigan:
Zondervan

NIV Application Commentary
Grand Rapids, Michigan:
Zondervan

The New American Commentary
Nashville, Tennessee:
Broadman and Holman
Publishers

One-Volume Commentaries

Carson, D.A., France, R.T.,
Motyer, J.A., & Wenham, G.J. Ed.
*New Bible Commentary: 21st
Century Edition*
Downers Grove, Illinois:
Inter-Varsity Press

Rydelnik, M.,.
Vanlaningham, M., Ed.
The Moody Bible Commentary
Chicago, Illinois: Moody
Publishers

We'd Love to Hear From You!

If you found this study helpful please take
a moment to share your thoughts.

Leave a Review

https://www.pamgillaspieshop.com/products/i-john-a-message-from-god

OR

Take a Short Survey

https://bit.ly/SolidTruthBookSurvey

www.ingramcontent.com/pod-product-compliance
Lightning Source LLC
Chambersburg PA
CBHW071525120626
46550CB00006B/2366